LET'S-READ-AND-FIND-OUT SCIENCE®

STAGE 2

DAY LIGHT, NIGHT LIGHT

Where Light Comes From

by Franklyn M. Branley

illustrated by Stacey Schuett

HarperCollins*Publishers*

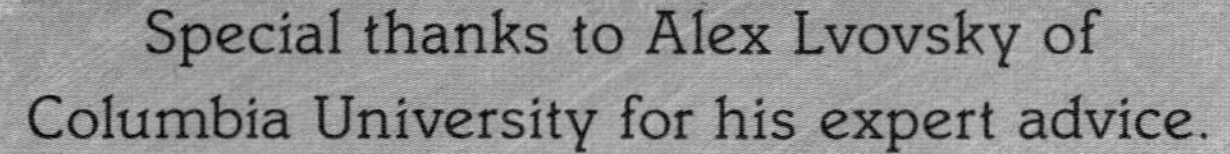

Special thanks to Alex Lvovsky of
Columbia University for his expert advice.

The illustrations for this book were done in acrylic and ink on Rives BFK paper.

The *Let's-Read-and-Find-Out Science* book series was originated by Dr. Franklyn M. Branley, Astronomer Emeritus and former Chairman of the American Museum–Hayden Planetarium, and was formerly co-edited by him and Dr. Roma Gans, Professor Emeritus of Childhood Education, Teachers College, Columbia University. Text and illustrations for each of the books in the series are checked for accuracy by an expert in the relevant field. For more information about Let's-Read-and-Find-Out Science books, write to HarperCollins Children's Books, 10 East 53rd Street, New York, NY 10022, or visit our web site at http://www.harperchildrens.com.

DAY LIGHT, NIGHT LIGHT

Library of Congress Cataloging-in-Publication Data
Branley, Franklyn Mansfield, date
Day light, night light : where light comes from / by Franklyn M. Branley ; illustrated by Stacey Schuett. — Rev. ed.
p. cm. — (Let's-read-and-find-out science. Stage 2)
Summary: Discusses the properties of light, particularly its source in heat.
ISBN 0-06-027294-5. — ISBN 0-06-027295-3 (lib. bdg.)
ISBN 0-06-445171-2 (pbk.)
1. Light—Juvenile literature. [1. Light.] I. Schuett, Stacey, ill. II. Title. III. Series.
QC360.B7 1998 96-33316
535—dc20 CIP
AC

Typography by Elynn Cohen
1 2 3 4 5 6 7 8 9 10
❖
Newly Illustrated Edition, 1998

DAY LIGHT, NIGHT LIGHT

Where Light Comes From

In the morning when you wake up, there is sunlight. Maybe it's cloudy and you can't see the sun. But it really is shining. If you were flying above the clouds, you could see the sun.

In the daytime there is light. That's because the sun is shining on your part of the Earth.

Even at night when you go to bed, there is light. There may be bright moonlight. Even if the moon isn't out, there may be light from the street, or from cars or other houses.

There is light around you all the time.

When it's dark inside, you turn on a light.

When it's dark outside, the streetlights come on. Or you turn on a flashlight.

Even when all these lights are off, there is still some light. It's hard to find a place that is really dark.

Sunlight comes from the sun. The sun is very hot. It sends out light to us.

Starlight comes from the stars. The stars are also very hot. They send out light to us.

Light comes from things that are very hot. The flame of a candle is hot. The little bulb in a flashlight is hot. And the big bulb in a lamp is hot. We call these hot things light sources, because light comes from them. Hot things make light.

A nail doesn't make light. But suppose there were some way you could heat a nail to make it get hotter and hotter. The nail would get so hot, it would produce light. First there would be a red glow in the room. When the nail got hotter, it would produce yellow light, and then light that was almost white. The hotter the nail got, the more light it would make. That is just what happens inside an electric light bulb. When you turn on the switch, little wires inside the bulb get hot. They get so hot that they send out a lot of light.

We see things when they get hot enough to make light. But most of the things that we see—chairs, people, trees, grass, rocks, books—are not hot. They do not send out their own light. We see them because light from the sun, or a candle, or a light bulb falls on them.

When light falls on something, it bounces off again, like a rubber ball. When light bounces off something, we say it is reflected, or turned around. When light bounces off something and is sent to us, we see that object.

We see trees and grass, rocks and birds, because sunlight falls on them. They reflect sunlight to us. We see the moon because sunlight falls on it. The moon reflects sunlight to us. The moon does not make its own light. Moonlight is reflected sunlight.

Light from the sun also falls on Venus and Mars and the other planets. The planets and the moon are not hot like stars. They are not light makers. We see the planets because they reflect sunlight to us. Astronauts in space see the Earth because the Earth reflects sunlight to them.

Look around you. How many things do you see that send out their own light? If it is daytime, you will probably see only one main kind of light—light from the sun. If it is nighttime, you might see the light from light bulbs. Or you might see a candle flame, a campfire, a flashlight, or the stars.

How many things do you see that *reflect* light? Probably hundreds of them. We see most things because they reflect light.

TOYS

Light travels very fast. You can see this when you turn on a lamp at night. All at once the whole room is filled with light. Point a flashlight at a tree far away. As soon as you turn on the light, you can see the tree.

Light travels so fast, it can go from the moon to the Earth and back in three seconds. If you could travel that fast, you could go around the world seven times in one second.

Light is just about everywhere. Probably you've never been in a place where there wasn't some light.

A dark room seems very dark at first. But after a while you can see things, because there is almost always a little light in every room. Try this experiment:

Take a white dish into a room and put it down. Then turn out the light. At first you won't see the dish. Your eyes have to adjust to the darkness. That means your pupils open wider so they can let in more light. Then your eyes can use other light sources, like the streetlight outside.

Pretty soon you may see the white dish. Pull the shades all the way down to make it darker. Maybe you can't see the dish now. But you can probably see where the windows are because of the streetlight.

It would be darker under your covers on a dark night. Or inside a dark closet in a dark room on a dark night. Maybe there would be no light at all. That would be real darkness.

There would also be real darkness in a cellar with no windows. Or a cave deep under the ground would be really dark. Maybe you can think of other places where it would be really dark.

Our world is full of light that comes to us from things that are hot. Most of our light comes from the hot sun. But we get some light from other hot things—candles and electric lights.

All during the day there is sunlight, even on a cloudy day. At night, too, the Earth is lit by the sun. People say it is lit by moonlight. But you know now that the moon does not make its own light—moonlight is reflected sunlight. Almost everything we see—books, trees, houses, cars, people, bugs, and birds—reflects light to us. Without light we could see nothing at all.